LANTERN COOKERY CLASSICS

KYLIE KWONG

LANTERN
an imprint of
PENGUIN BOOKS

SEAFOOD

MEAT AND POULTRY

EGGS, VEGETABLES AND TOFU

RICE, DUMPLINGS AND NOODLES

STOCKS, SAUCES AND SALTS

SEAFOOD

Sweet corn and crabmeat soup

Here the sweet, crunchy corn niblets and the freshest, sweetest crabmeat combine to create a wholesome and comforting soup.

4 cobs of sweet corn
2 tablespoons peanut oil
1 white onion, finely diced
2 tablespoons finely sliced ginger
1 garlic clove, finely diced
1 teaspoon sea salt
½ cup (125 ml) shaohsing wine or dry sherry
1.75 litres Rich Chinese Chicken Stock
    (see page 130)
200 g fresh crabmeat
1½ teaspoons light soy sauce
2 free-range eggs, lightly beaten
1 tablespoon finely sliced spring onion
small pinch ground white pepper

1 Remove kernels from corn cobs by running a sharp knife down the sides of each cob – you should have about 3 cups of corn kernels.

2 Heat oil in a heavy-based saucepan and gently fry onion, ginger, garlic and salt for 5 minutes. Add shaohsing or sherry and simmer until it has reduced by half. Stir in corn and stock, bring to the boil and simmer gently for 30 minutes. You may need to skim the soup occasionally to remove any impurities.

3 Stir through crabmeat and soy sauce, then lower heat and slowly pour the beaten eggs into the soup in a thin stream, stirring constantly with a fork. Remove soup from heat as soon as you see the eggs forming fine 'ribbons'.

4 Serve the soup in bowls, garnished with spring onion and pepper.

Mussel salad with egg, tarragon and pickled cucumber

SERVE AS A STARTER FOR 4

This French-inspired salad is one of my all-time favourite recipes. The mussels are just barely cooked, so they remain juicy, plump and salty – absolutely gorgeous. The pickled cucumber is simple to make but intriguingly complex. It adds a lovely depth of flavour to the salad, along with the unmistakeable, slightly aniseedy note of tarragon. The boiled egg somehow brings the whole dish down to earth and balances the delicate textures of the mussels, herbs and cucumber.

750 g live mussels
2 garlic cloves, crushed
2 tablespoons extra virgin olive oil
sea salt
1 tablespoon roughly chopped tarragon
2 tablespoons roughly chopped
flat-leaf parsley
4 hard-boiled free-range eggs
pinch cracked white pepper

STOCK
2 cups (500 ml) Rich Chinese Chicken
Stock (see page 130)
2 cups (500 ml) white wine
1 spring onion, trimmed and sliced
¼ bunch flat-leaf parsley,
cut in half crossways
1 teaspoon sea salt
1 teaspoon white sugar
1 teaspoon white peppercorns
4 bay leaves

PICKLED CUCUMBER
1 cucumber, peeled
¼ cup (60 ml) chardonnay vinegar
1 teaspoon sea salt
1 teaspoon white sugar

1 Scrub, debeard, rinse and drain the mussels. Place all stock ingredients in a medium-sized, heavy-based saucepan and bring to the boil. Reduce heat and simmer, uncovered, until reduced by half. Increase heat and add mussels, stirring well to combine. As the mussels begin to open, immediately remove from pan with tongs and place in a bowl; discard any that do not open. (Take care not to overcook the mussels.) Remove the meat from the shells and set aside. Continue simmering remaining stock over medium heat for a further 25 minutes, or until reduced by half again and richer in flavour.

2 Meanwhile, make the pickled cucumber. Cut cucumber in half lengthways and scoop out seeds. Place cut-side down on a chopping board and cut on the diagonal into 5 mm slices. Place in a bowl and combine with vinegar, salt and sugar. Cover and refrigerate for at least 1 hour.

3 Pound garlic, half the oil and a little sea salt with a mortar and pestle until you have a coarse paste. Gently stir into reserved mussel meat, along with herbs and a scant ¼ cup (60 ml) of reduced stock. Combine this with pickled cucumber.

4 Slice and arrange eggs on a platter. Top with mussel and cucumber mixture, sprinkle with pepper and drizzle with remaining oil.

King prawn toasts

This recipe is so cool! What is wacky about this dish is that you think to yourself, 'How does the prawn mixture stay on the bread slices once it is lowered into the hot oil?' Well, all I can say is follow the recipe, roll the toasts in sesame seeds on both sides, and see for yourself – it is like MAGIC!!!

As children we always felt it was a bit of a treat when Mum served king prawn toasts, as they were usually reserved for special occasions. They are definitely a crowd-pleaser, and most impressive. I like to serve them with a pungent, sweet and spicy dipping sauce.

16 uncooked king prawns
2 spring onions, finely chopped
small handful of finely chopped coriander
1 tablespoon finely sliced ginger
2 teaspoons shaohsing wine or dry sherry
1 teaspoon light soy sauce
1 free-range egg white, lightly beaten
½ teaspoon sea salt
6 slices thick white bread
¼ cup (35 g) sesame seeds
vegetable oil for deep-frying

SWEET CHILLI AND CARROT DIPPING SAUCE
½ small carrot, peeled
½ teaspoon white sugar
½ teaspoon sea salt
2 cups (500 ml) rice wine vinegar
1½ cups (330 g) white sugar, extra
100 ml fish sauce
2 large red chillies, finely sliced on the diagonal

1 To make the sauce, finely slice carrot lengthways into ribbons using a vegetable peeler. Cut ribbons into thin strips. Combine carrot in a bowl with sugar and salt, mix well and leave to stand for 10 minutes. Drain carrot and, using your hands, gently squeeze away any excess liquid.

2 Meanwhile, place vinegar and extra sugar in a medium-sized, heavy-based saucepan and bring to the boil. Reduce heat and simmer, uncovered, for about 15 minutes or until reduced by almost half and slightly syrupy. Remove from heat, ladle into bowl of pickled carrots, fish sauce and chilli and set aside.

3 Peel and devein the prawns, then cut prawn meat into 1.5 cm dice. In a bowl, combine prawn meat with remaining ingredients except bread, sesame seeds and oil, and mix well.

4 Remove and discard crusts from bread and cut each slice in half. Place a tablespoon of prawn mixture on each piece of bread, lightly pressing to cover well. Gently roll each piece of prawn bread in sesame seeds to coat lightly.

5 Heat oil in a hot wok until the surface seems to shimmer slightly. Working in batches, carefully lower prawn toasts, prawn-side down, into hot oil. Deep-fry over medium heat for 1 minute. Turn toasts over and cook other side for a further minute, or until lightly browned all over and just cooked through. Remove from wok using a slotted spoon and drain on kitchen paper.

6 Serve immediately with a bowl of sweet chilli and carrot dipping sauce.

Kingfish sashimi with Mathew Lindsay's dressing

Mathew Lindsay was my head chef at Billy Kwong for several years, and his talent, creativity and instinctive feel for cooking are outstanding. We work together so well. I really love making connections with food producers, and I'll often return from the local markets with a particular ingredient I'd like to offer in the restaurant. Matt then takes it from there, coming up with the finer details of the dish. There is a natural synergy between us that I find refreshing and fulfilling. Matty came up with this gorgeous dressing for our sashimi of kingfish, and it has since become a menu staple. You could also use sashimi-grade snapper, sea bass, ocean trout or tuna.

500 g sashimi-grade yellowtail kingfish fillet
Sichuan Pepper and Salt (see page 138)

DRESSING
⅓ cup (80 ml) brown rice vinegar
¼ cup (40 g) brown sugar
¼ cup (60 ml) water
⅓ cup (80 ml) tamari
1 tablespoon sesame oil
1 tablespoon extra virgin olive oil
1 tablespoon finely grated ginger
1 tablespoon finely grated white onion

1 Using a very sharp knife, cut fish into 5 mm slices and arrange on a platter.

2 To make the dressing, pour vinegar into a heatproof bowl. Place sugar and water in a small saucepan and bring to the boil, then turn heat down to medium and allow to caramelise until dark brown – this will take approximately 5 minutes. Just before caramel begins to smoke, remove from heat, quickly pour into vinegar bowl and whisk well. Add tamari and sesame oil and whisk well again. Add olive oil and whisk well, then stir through ginger and onion.

3 Drizzle dressing over kingfish, sprinkle with Sichuan pepper and salt, and serve immediately.

Salad of king prawns, avocado and watercress

Prawn and avocados are a well-loved combination. Be sure to use the freshest bunch of watercress to liven up this salad. The honey and tamari dressing, with its nectar-like quality, coats the avocado and prawns perfectly.

12 uncooked king prawns
1 tablespoon extra virgin olive oil
1 ripe avocado
½ bunch watercress, washed and trimmed
freshly ground black pepper

HONEY AND TAMARI DRESSING

2 tablespoons honey
2 tablespoons tamari
¼ cup (60 ml) extra virgin olive oil
juice of 1 lemon

1 Peel and devein the prawns, but leave the tail intact. Butterfly the prawns by making a shallow cut along the back – this helps them to cook quickly and evenly.

2 Place prawns in a single layer in a shallow heatproof bowl that will fit inside a steamer basket. Drizzle with oil, then place bowl inside steamer and position over a deep saucepan or wok of boiling water. Steam, covered, for about 5 minutes or until prawns are just cooked through. Carefully remove bowl from steamer and transfer prawns to another bowl so they don't overcook in the residual heat, then set aside.

3 Cut avocado in half lengthways and remove seed. Using a large spoon, scoop out the flesh from each half and cut into slices.

4 To make the dressing, place all ingredients in a bowl and whisk well.

5 Arrange watercress on a serving platter with avocado. Place cooked prawns on top, drizzle with dressing and serve.

Steamed whole snapper with ginger and spring onions

This dish shows how well steaming preserves purity of flavour and texture. The naturally sweet, delicate and moist flesh of the snapper combines with the aromatic ingredients to create a beautifully balanced, subtle, clean and salty flavour.

Other types of whole fish suitable for this recipe are bream, King George whiting, silver perch, Murray perch, pigfish, coral trout, red emperor and barramundi.

1 × 750 g whole snapper, scaled,
    cleaned and gutted
1 leaf Chinese white cabbage,
    cut into 4 squares
¼ cup (60 ml) Rich Chinese Chicken
    Stock (see page 130)
¼ cup (60 ml) shaohsing wine or dry sherry
⅓ cup finely sliced ginger
2 teaspoons white sugar
3½ tablespoons light soy sauce
¼ teaspoon sesame oil
3 spring onions, cut into fine julienne strips
¼ cup (60 ml) peanut oil
½ bunch coriander, leaves only
small pinch ground white pepper

1 Pat fish dry with kitchen paper and place on a chopping board. With a sharp knife, make three diagonal slits into one side of the fish, then score in the opposite direction to make a diamond pattern. Turn fish over and repeat on other side.

2 Bring a large steamer pot of water to the boil. Arrange cabbage squares in a shallow heatproof bowl and place fish on top. Pour combined stock and shaohsing or sherry over fish, then sprinkle with half the ginger, avoiding the head. Place bowl inside steamer basket over boiling water, put lid on steamer and steam for 10–12 minutes or until fish is cooked. The flesh should be white through to the bone; if it is still translucent, replace lid firmly and steam for another minute or so.

3 Remove steamer basket from steamer, then carefully remove bowl from steamer basket. Sprinkle sugar evenly over fish, avoiding the head. Drizzle fish with combined soy sauce and sesame oil, then sprinkle with remaining ginger and half the spring onion.

4 In a small saucepan, heat peanut oil until it reaches smoking point. (This is the most important point of the dish – the oil must be hot enough to 'scald' the ginger and spring onion.) Slowly and carefully drizzle hot oil over fish. Garnish with remaining spring onion, coriander and pepper, and serve immediately.

Blue eye and king prawns with lemon and honey onions

The combination of salty, sweet and sour flavours is evident in so many cuisines – Asian, Middle Eastern, European – and it's a trio of tastes that I adore. In this recipe, the lemon and honey onions work as a beautiful relish for the delicate flavours of the prawns and fish.

In cooler climes, haddock or cod can be substituted for the blue eye.

16 uncooked king prawns
pinch sea salt and cracked pepper
400 g blue eye fillet, cut into large pieces
1 oxheart tomato, roughly sliced
small handful of chopped flat-leaf parsley

STOCK
3 garlic cloves
8 slices ginger
1 tablespoon sea salt
½ cup (125 ml) olive oil
1 stick of celery, sliced
1 small carrot, peeled and finely diced
1½ tablespoons sliced lemongrass
2 vine-ripened tomatoes, sliced
small handful of flat-leaf parsley leaves,
    cut in half crossways
½ cup (125 ml) white wine

LEMON AND HONEY ONIONS
1½ tablespoons extra virgin olive oil
10 small salad onions, trimmed
1 small red onion, sliced
½ teaspoon sea salt
2 tablespoons honey
1 tablespoon lemon juice

1 Peel and devein the prawns, but leave the tail intact. Reserve heads and shells for stock. Butterfly the prawns by making a shallow cut along the back – this helps them to cook quickly and evenly.

2 To make the stock, pound garlic, ginger and salt with a mortar and pestle until you have a fine paste. Heat oil in a small heavy-based saucepan, add garlic paste, celery, carrot and lemongrass, and gently fry for 2 minutes, or until aromatic. Stir in tomatoes and parsley, then add reserved prawn heads and shells and gently fry for 1 minute. Pour in wine and simmer for 2 minutes, or until alcohol has evaporated. Add 1 cup (250 ml) of water and simmer, uncovered, for 20 minutes. Have ready a fine strainer over a large bowl. Ladle stock into strainer, gently pressing the ingredients to extract as much liquid as possible. Set aside.

3 For the onions, heat oil in a frying pan and add onions and salt. Gently fry for about 2 minutes, or until onions are lightly browned. Add honey, reduce heat and simmer gently over low heat for 2 minutes. Add lemon juice and simmer, uncovered, for about 10 minutes, or until slightly thickened and caramelised.

4 Season prawns with a little salt and pepper, and cook in a heated, oiled frying pan until lightly browned and just tender. Remove prawns from pan and cover with foil to keep warm while you poach the fish.

5 Return stock to a small saucepan and bring to the boil; add fish pieces and reduce heat. Poach very gently, uncovered, for about 3 minutes, or until just tender. Place sliced tomato in the centre of a large, shallow bowl and arrange prawns and fish on top. Spoon over stock and top with onions. Garnish with parsley and serve immediately.

Deep-fried whole fish with sweet and sour sauce

The sauce that traditionally accompanies sweet and sour pork is equally delicious with deep-fried whole fish; while its intensity would overwhelm a steamed dish, it perfectly offsets the richness of deep-fried food. The base for the sauce can be made in advance, so all you need to do is toss in the soy sauce, tomato and cucumber just before serving. Suitable fish for this recipe include snapper, bream, barramundi, sand whiting, ocean perch, cod, halibut and sea bass.

1 × 750 g whole fish, scaled, cleaned and gutted
vegetable oil for deep-frying
3 spring onions, finely chopped, to garnish

SWEET AND SOUR SAUCE
⅓ cup (80 ml) rice wine vinegar
2 tablespoons white sugar
½ teaspoon sea salt
2 tablespoons shaohsing wine or dry sherry
1 tablespoon finely sliced ginger
1 small carrot, peeled and finely diced
1 tablespoon light soy sauce
1 small tomato, finely diced
**½ small cucumber, sliced into ribbons using
    a vegetable peeler**

1 To make the sauce, combine vinegar, sugar, salt, shaohsing or sherry and ginger in a small heavy-based saucepan and stir over heat until sugar dissolves. Add carrot and simmer, uncovered, for 2 minutes. Remove from heat and set aside.

2 Pat fish dry with kitchen paper and place on a chopping board. With a sharp knife, make four diagonal slits into one side of the fish, then score in the opposite direction to make a diamond pattern. Turn fish over and repeat on other side.

3 Heat oil in a hot wok until the surface seems to shimmer slightly. Carefully lower fish into the wok so it is completely covered by oil. Fry for 3 minutes, then carefully turn fish and fry for a further 3 minutes or until fish is lightly browned and just cooked through when tested. The flesh should be white through to the bone; if it is still translucent, cook for another minute or so. Using a spatula, carefully remove fish from wok and drain on kitchen paper.

4 Finally, gently reheat sweet and sour sauce. Stir in soy sauce, tomato and cucumber and remove from heat.

5 Transfer fish to a large platter, spoon over warm sweet and sour sauce, garnish with chopped spring onion and serve immediately.

Soy sauce fish fillets

With its hints of aniseed, cinnamon, soy, ginger, garlic and orange, red master stock is wonderfully intense and interesting. Lightly poached in the stock, fillets of fish gain depth and complexity of flavour. Suggested fish for this recipe include salmon, ocean trout, blue eye, Murray cod, red emperor, mahi mahi, barramundi, halibut or sea bass.

4 × 100 g fish fillets
1 bunch bok choy, cored and cut into
**   four crossways**

RED MASTER STOCK
1.5 litres cold water
¾ cup (180 ml) shaohsing wine or dry sherry
½ cup (125 ml) dark soy sauce
¼ cup (60 ml) light soy sauce
½ cup (110 g) brown sugar
3 garlic cloves, crushed
¼ cup finely sliced ginger
2 spring onions, trimmed and cut in
**   half crossways**
¼ teaspoon sesame oil
2 star anise
1 cinnamon quill
2 strips fresh orange zest

1 Place all stock ingredients in a wide deep frying pan – about 30 cm wide × 5 cm deep – and bring to the boil. Reduce heat and simmer gently for 40 minutes to allow flavours to infuse.

2 Lower fish into simmering stock and cover with a piece of baking paper cut to the same size as the pan to ensure it is fully submerged. Poach fish gently for exactly 2 minutes; there should be no more than an occasional ripple breaking the surface. Immediately remove pan from the heat and allow fish to steep in the stock for 5 minutes to complete the cooking process.

3 Add bok choy to a saucepan of boiling salted water and blanch for 30 seconds or until almost tender. Drain immediately.

4 Using a slotted spoon, gently remove fish from stock and transfer to a serving bowl. Spoon ⅔ cup (160 ml) of the master stock, along with some whole spices and aromatics, over fish. Top with bok choy and serve immediately.

Stir-fried king prawns with green asparagus and baby corn

There is no substitute for the delicious, earthy, flavour of fresh baby corn, which ensures the unique character of this dish.

Sweet succulent prawns, crunchy green asparagus, grassy-tasting baby corn and velvety-textured black fungus make for a light, clean, refreshing and healthy dish!

12 uncooked king prawns
4 spears green asparagus
¼ cup (60 ml) peanut oil
1 tablespoon finely sliced ginger
4 spears fresh baby corn
2 tablespoons shaohsing wine or dry sherry
¼ teaspoon white sugar
1 tablespoon light soy sauce
¼ teaspoon sesame oil
¼ cup (60 ml) Rich Chinese Chicken
    Stock (see page 130)
50 g finely sliced fresh black cloud ear fungus
¼ teaspoon black vinegar
1 tablespoon roughly chopped pak chii farang
    (sawtooth coriander)

1 Peel and devein the prawns, but leave the tail intact. Butterfly the prawns by making a shallow cut along the back – this helps them to cook quickly and evenly. Trim woody ends from asparagus spears and slice into 5 cm lengths on the diagonal.

2 Heat peanut oil in a hot wok and stir-fry prawns for 1 minute. Add ginger, asparagus and baby corn and stir-fry for 1 minute. Pour in shaohsing or sherry and simmer for 10 seconds. Add sugar, soy sauce and sesame oil and stir-fry for 20 seconds. Add stock, then simmer for 2 minutes or until prawns are just tender. Finally, add cloud ear fungus, vinegar and pak chii farang. Stir to combine, then serve immediately.

Prawn and mint salad

This dish is all about simplicity and freshness. Lightly poach the prawns, throw in finely sliced vegetables and mint, then combine with a vibrant dressing for a perfect light summer meal.

16 cooked prawns
1 small carrot, peeled
1 cucumber, peeled
½ iceberg lettuce, finely shredded
1 stick of celery, finely sliced on the diagonal
6 spring onions, cut into fine julienne strips
small handful of roughly torn mint

DRESSING
¼ cup (60 ml) extra virgin olive oil
2 tablespoons malt vinegar
2 tablespoons light soy sauce
2 teaspoons white sugar

1 Peel and devein the prawns and set aside.

2 Using a vegetable peeler, finely slice carrot lengthways into ribbons. Cut cucumber in half lengthways and scoop out the seeds using a spoon. Place cut-side down on a chopping board and finely slice on the diagonal.

3 To make the dressing, place all ingredients in a small bowl and stir to combine.

4 In a separate bowl, combine prawns, carrot and cucumber with remaining ingredients. Pour over dressing and toss well.

5 Arrange salad on a platter and serve immediately.

Stir-fried squid with garlic and chilli

SERVE AS A MEAL FOR 4 WITH STEAMED RICE
OR AS PART OF A BANQUET FOR 4–6

This dish encapsulates the essence of Chinese cuisine – harmony and balance between flavour, texture and ingredients. The scoring of the squid makes it curl on contact with the hot oil, while also allowing the flavours to penetrate. Because all the ingredients are finely chopped, you must keep the wok moving at all times, stirring constantly, to prevent burning. The addition of lime juice at the end gives the dish a burst of freshness.

**600 g squid, cleaned and scored (ask your
    fishmonger to do this for you)**
2 tablespoons vegetable oil
2 tablespoons finely diced ginger
4 garlic cloves, finely diced
2 large red chillies, finely sliced on the diagonal
2 tablespoons shaohsing wine or dry sherry
2 tablespoons water
2 teaspoons white sugar
2 teaspoons sea salt
9 spring onions, finely chopped
2 teaspoons lime juice
2 limes, halved
**2 large red chillies, finely sliced
    on the diagonal, to garnish**

1 Heat half the oil in a hot wok until the surface seems to shimmer slightly. Add half the squid and stir-fry for 30 seconds. Remove from wok with a slotted spoon and set aside. Add remaining oil to the hot wok, toss in remaining squid and stir-fry for 30 seconds.

2 Return reserved squid to wok with ginger, garlic and chilli and stir-fry for 30 seconds, stirring constantly to ensure garlic does not burn. Add shaohsing or sherry, water, sugar and salt and stir-fry for 20 seconds.

3 Toss in spring onion and stir-fry for a further minute or until squid is just cooked through. Finally, add lime juice and remove from heat.

4 Arrange squid on a platter, garnish with chilli and serve immediately with lime halves.

Steamed baby crabs stir-fried with ginger and spring onions

If baby crabs are unavailable for this just use regular crabs chopped into quarters – your fishmonger should be able to do this for you – and increase the steaming time to 5–7 minutes. When the crab is ready, the meat should be white rather than translucent.

6 × 150 g baby crabs
2 tablespoons peanut oil
5 cm piece ginger, cut into thin strips
3 spring onions, trimmed and finely sliced
2 garlic cloves, roughly chopped
2 tablespoons light soy sauce
2 tablespoons finely chopped coriander
    roots and stems
1 teaspoon brown sugar
½ teaspoon sesame oil

1 Clean baby crabs by lifting up the top shell and removing the furry grey gills from each side.

2 Wash crabs well, cut in half widthways and place in a shallow heatproof bowl that will fit inside a steamer basket. Place bowl inside steamer and position over a deep saucepan or wok of boiling water. Steam, covered, for 3 minutes. Remove crabs from steamer basket and drain well.

3 Heat peanut oil in a hot wok until the surface seems to shimmer slightly. Add ginger, spring onion and garlic and stir-fry for 1 minute. Add crabs and stir-fry for 30 seconds. Add remaining ingredients and stir-fry for a further minute. Serve immediately.

Steamed mussels with tomato and Sichuan chilli oil

This recipe combines Italian techniques with Chinese ingredients. I really feel that the Chinese and the Italians share a similar approach to cooking seafood, cooking it lightly and throwing in a lot of herbs at the end to keep the flavours fresh and lively.

2 kg live mussels
4 tomatoes, roughly chopped
2 bunches mint, leaves picked
1 bunch coriander, leaves picked
4 spring onions, cut into fine julienne strips
1 teaspoon Sichuan Pepper and
    Salt (see page 138)

SICHUAN CHILLI OIL
1 tablespoon dried chilli flakes
1 cup (250 ml) safflower or sunflower oil
⅓ cup (80 ml) tamari
⅓ cup (80 ml) hot stock or water
2 tablespoons brown rice vinegar
2 tablespoons brown sugar

1 To make the Sichuan chilli oil, place chilli flakes in a heatproof bowl. Heat oil in a small heavy-based frying pan until the surface seems to shimmer slightly. Carefully pour hot oil over chilli in the bowl to release heat and flavour. Stir to combine and stand uncovered for 30 minutes. Strain oil mixture through a fine sieve over a bowl and discard half the chilli flakes remaining in sieve. Whisk in the other half of the chilli flakes, along with the rest of the ingredients. Set aside.

2 Scrub, debeard, rinse and drain the mussels. Put half the mussels in a wok with 1 cup (250 ml) of water. Place over high heat, cover, and steam until shells open. As the mussels begin to open, immediately remove from wok with tongs and place in a bowl. Clean the wok, add fresh water and the second batch of mussels. Discard any mussels that do not open.

3 Combine drained mussels, tomatoes, herbs, spring onions and Sichuan chilli oil in a bowl. Toss thoroughly, garnish with Sichuan pepper and salt and serve immediately.

MEAT AND POULTRY

Roast Wagyu beef fillet with sweet and sour red radish salad

The caramel texture and rich flavours of this marinade are perfectly complemented by the sweet and sour radish salad. Because the beef is served quite rare, use the best-quality fillet you can find.

2 × 200 g Wagyu beef fillets
2 tablespoons vegetable oil
dash of extra virgin olive oil

MARINADE

2 tablespoons kecap manis
½ cup (125 ml) shaohsing wine or dry sherry
1 tablespoon white sugar
½ tablespoon sesame oil
2 tablespoons light soy sauce
2 tablespoons Chinese black vinegar

SWEET AND SOUR RADISH SALAD

3 garlic cloves, peeled
1 tablespoon extra virgin olive oil
4 red radishes, finely sliced
1 small red onion, finely sliced
¼ cup (60 ml) red wine vinegar
2 teaspoons white sugar
1 tablespoon sea salt

1 Combine all marinade ingredients in a large bowl, then add beef and mix well. Cover and refrigerate for 3 hours.

2 To make the salad, crush garlic with a mortar and pestle, add oil and grind into a paste. Transfer paste to a bowl and combine with all remaining ingredients. Cover and refrigerate for 1 hour.

3 Preheat oven to 220°C. Remove beef from marinade and drain; discard marinade. Heat vegetable oil in a heavy-based frying pan. Cook beef for about 2 minutes, or until well browned on one side. Turn over and briefly seal other side, then remove immediately.

4 Transfer beef to a roasting tin and cook for about 4 minutes, or until rare. Remove from oven, loosely cover with foil and leave to rest in a warm place for 10 minutes.

5 To serve, cut beef into 1 cm-thick slices and arrange on a platter. Top with sweet and sour radish salad and drizzle with a little olive oil.

Stir-fried beef with black bean and chilli sauce

This is a classic Cantonese dish, with a versatile sauce that suits many meats, fish, seafood and tofu. I like it because it is so colourful and vibrant. Add more chilli if you like it extra hot!

600 g beef fillet, cut into 1 cm slices
⅓ cup (80 ml) vegetable oil
¼ cup finely chopped spring onion

MARINADE

2 tablespoons shaohsing wine or dry sherry
1 teaspoon sea salt
1 teaspoon white sugar

BLACK BEAN AND CHILLI SAUCE

1 small red onion, finely sliced
¼ cup finely sliced ginger
3 garlic cloves, roughly chopped
1 tablespoon salted black beans
2 tablespoons shaohsing wine or dry sherry
1 tablespoon white sugar
1 tablespoon light soy sauce
2 tablespoons oyster sauce
1 tablespoon malt vinegar
½ teaspoon sesame oil
2 large red chillies, finely sliced on the diagonal
½ red capsicum (pepper), seeds and membrane
  removed, thinly sliced

1 Combine all marinade ingredients in a large bowl, then add beef and mix well. Cover and refrigerate for 30 minutes.

2 Heat half the oil in a hot wok until the surface seems to shimmer slightly. Add half the marinated beef and stir-fry for 30 seconds. Remove from wok with a slotted spoon and set aside. Add remaining beef and stir-fry for 30 seconds, then remove from wok and set aside.

3 Meanwhile, make the black bean and chilli sauce. Add remaining oil to hot wok. Add onion, ginger, garlic and black beans and stir-fry over high heat for 30 seconds, stirring constantly to ensure the black beans do not burn.

4 Return beef to the wok with shaohsing or sherry and stir-fry for 30 seconds. Add sugar, soy sauce, oyster sauce, vinegar and sesame oil and stir-fry for a further minute. Lastly, add chilli and capsicum and stir-fry for a further 30 seconds.

5 To serve, arrange beef on a platter and garnish with spring onion.

Marinated rare roast beef with ginger dressing

SERVE AS PART OF A BANQUET FOR 4–6

This refreshing ginger dressing offsets the beef's richness perfectly. As the beef is served quite rare, use the best-quality grass-fed fillet of beef you can find – your reward will be tender, flavoursome meat.

600 g beef fillet, in one piece

MARINADE
2 garlic cloves, finely chopped
2.5 cm piece ginger, finely chopped
¼ cup (60 ml) shaohsing wine or dry sherry
2 tablespoons tamari or light soy sauce
2 tablespoons brown sugar
1 teaspoon sesame oil

DRESSING
1 spring onion, finely sliced
5 cm piece ginger, finely chopped
2 tablespoons finely sliced coriander stems
1 tablespoon brown sugar
2 tablespoons brown rice vinegar
2 tablespoons tamari or light soy sauce
¼ cup (60 ml) extra virgin olive oil

1 Preheat oven to 180°C.

2 Combine all marinade ingredients in a bowl, then add beef and mix well. Cover and refrigerate for 1 hour.

3 Remove beef from marinade and sear on a hot chargrill plate or in a heavy-based frying pan for 3 minutes on each side. Transfer beef to an oven tray and roast for approximately 12 minutes (for rare). Remove from oven, then loosely cover beef and oven tray with foil and leave to rest in a warm place for 15 minutes.

4 Meanwhile, make the dressing. Combine all ingredients in a bowl and mix thoroughly.

5 To serve, cut beef into 1 cm-thick slices and arrange on a platter. Pour over dressing and serve while still warm, or at room temperature.

Dry-fried Sichuan beef

For this dish, the beef fillets are semi-frozen before cutting, which allows you to slice them into super-fine strips without tearing. The finished dish is filled with interesting textures; it has no 'sauce' but is deliciously crunchy, salty and spicy all at once.

2 × 300 g beef fillets
1½ cups (375 ml) vegetable oil
1 tablespoon vegetable oil, extra
2 large red chillies, finely sliced on the diagonal
1 tablespoon finely diced ginger
3 garlic cloves, finely diced
2 tablespoons hoisin sauce
2 teaspoons Sichuan Pepper and
    Salt (see page 138)
9 spring onions, finely chopped
pinch Sichuan Pepper and Salt
    (see page 138), extra
large handful of finely shredded iceberg lettuce

1 Wrap beef fillets in plastic wrap. Place on a tray in the freezer for about 30 minutes or until slightly firm. Remove plastic wrap and, using a sharp knife, cut beef fillets into 5 mm slices, then cut slices into 5 mm strips.

2 Heat oil in a hot wok until the surface seems to shimmer slightly. Add half the beef and stir-fry for 1 minute, stirring constantly to prevent beef sticking together. Remove from wok with a slotted spoon, drain well on kitchen paper and set aside. Repeat process with remaining beef. Remove excess oil from wok and wipe clean.

3 Heat extra oil in the same hot wok. Stir in chilli, ginger and garlic and cook over medium heat for 30 seconds, stirring constantly to ensure garlic does not burn. Return beef to the wok with hoisin sauce and stir-fry for a further 30 seconds. Add Sichuan pepper and salt and stir-fry for 30 seconds, then stir through the spring onion.

4 Arrange beef on a platter, sprinkle with extra Sichuan pepper and salt, and top with lettuce.

Sizzling beef

Anyone who's been to a Chinese restaurant in Australia knows there's always a dish on the menu called 'Sizzling beef'. It's generally surrounded by a heavy, thick sauce or marinade, which I find way too rich, and has a cardboardy, unnatural flavour. I've got no idea why people order it – maybe they get drawn in by the drama of it all, as the hissing and smoking cast-iron platter weaves its way to their table. My sizzling beef is a much more refined version, where the natural flavour of the meat really shines, lifted by some Sichuan pepper and salt and fresh lemon juice.

400 g top-quality beef fillet,
cut into 1.5 cm-thick slices
2 small white onions, peeled
2 tablespoons peanut oil, extra
6 cm piece ginger, very finely sliced
4 garlic cloves, crushed
1 tablespoon shaohsing wine or dry sherry
1 teaspoon kecap manis
1 ½ tablespoons mushroom soy sauce
¼ teaspoon sesame oil
pinch Sichuan Pepper and Salt (see page 138)
¼ cup (60 ml) lemon juice

MARINADE

2 tablespoons shaohsing wine or dry sherry
2 tablespoons Chinese barbecue sauce
(ideally Leung Cheung Woo brand)
1 tablespoon peanut oil
1 teaspoon white sugar
1 tablespoon mushroom soy sauce
¼ teaspoon sesame oil

1 Combine all marinade ingredients in a bowl, then add beef and mix well. Cover and refrigerate for 2 hours.

2 Cut onions in half, then cut into 2 cm wedges. Pull the wedges apart to separate the layers.

3 Heat peanut oil in a hot wok until the surface seems to shimmer slightly. Add onion, ginger and garlic and stir-fry for 1 minute. Add beef to wok, along with the marinade, and sear on one side for about 1 minute, or until lightly browned; do not stir-fry. Turn beef over and sear other side for a further minute. Add shaohsing or sherry, kecap manis, 1 tablespoon of soy sauce and sesame oil and stir-fry for 1 minute, or until the beef is just tender and the flavours are balanced.

4 Arrange beef on a platter, sprinkle with remaining soy sauce and Sichuan pepper and salt. Serve immediately with a small bowl of lemon juice on the side.

Sweet and sour pork

Marinating the pork overnight is a must for this dish – the flavour is so much more intense. The main difference between my sweet and sour sauce and traditional recipes is that I use fresh tomatoes instead of tomato sauce out of the bottle, and fresh pineapple instead of tinned pineapple.

1½ tablespoons cornflour
1 tablespoon cold water
2 × 300 g pork neck fillets, cut in half lengthways, then into bite-sized pieces on the diagonal
2 free-range egg yolks, lightly beaten
3 teaspoons light soy sauce
2 teaspoons sesame oil
1 teaspoon sea salt
¼ cup (35 g) plain flour
¼ cup (35 g) cornflour, extra
vegetable oil for deep-frying
1 tablespoon coriander leaves, to garnish
1 tablespoon spring onion, cut into fine julienne strips, to garnish

SWEET AND SOUR SAUCE
1 small carrot, peeled
1 small cucumber
¾ cup (180 ml) malt vinegar
100 ml shaohsing wine or dry sherry
½ cup (110 g) white sugar
1 teaspoon sea salt
4 garlic cloves, crushed
2 tablespoons finely sliced ginger
¼ small ripe pineapple, peeled, cored and finely sliced
½ yellow capsicum (pepper), finely sliced
2 small tomatoes, finely sliced
2 tablespoons light soy sauce

1 Blend cornflour with water in a medium-sized bowl until dissolved. Add pork, egg yolks, soy sauce, sesame oil and salt and mix well. Cover and leave to marinate in the refrigerator overnight.

2 To make the sweet and sour sauce, finely slice carrot into ribbons using a vegetable peeler. Set aside. Cut cucumber in half lengthways, slice on the diagonal and set aside.

3 Place vinegar, shaohsing or sherry, sugar and salt in a medium-sized heavy-based saucepan and stir over high heat until sugar dissolves. Bring to the boil and add garlic and ginger, then reduce heat and simmer, uncovered, for 10 minutes. Add carrot, cucumber, pineapple, capsicum and tomato and simmer for a further 3 minutes or until pineapple is tender and tomato has broken down slightly. Stir in soy sauce, then remove from heat and set aside.

4 Combine plain flour and extra cornflour. Add to the marinated pork and mix well. Heat vegetable oil in a hot wok until the surface seems to shimmer slightly. Deep-fry pork in batches over high heat for 1 minute, then reduce heat to medium and fry for another 2 minutes, or until pork is almost cooked through. Remove from wok and drain on kitchen paper. Gently reheat sweet and sour sauce.

5 Finally, return all pork to the hot wok and deep-fry for a further 3 minutes, or until lightly browned, crispy and cooked through. Remove from wok and drain well on kitchen paper.

6 Arrange pork on a platter, garnish with coriander and spring onion and serve immediately with a bowl of warm sweet and sour sauce.

Marinated pork spare ribs

No-one I know can resist a sticky caramelised pork rib. Rather than resorting to bottled sauces packed with artificial flavours and preservatives for the marinade, I like to use Spiral barley malt – its dark golden-brown colour, and thick and luscious texture is perfect here. The taste of this natural grain sweetener is similar to caramelised honey, so if you can't find it you could use honey or golden syrup instead. Marinate overnight, if you wish.

1 kg pork ribs
4 limes, cut in half

MARINADE
300 g barley malt
¼ cup (60 ml) tamari
¼ cup (60 ml) brown rice vinegar
¼ cup (60 ml) shaohsing wine or dry sherry
6 garlic cloves, crushed and roughly chopped
7 cm piece ginger, roughly chopped
1 tablespoon Sichuan peppercorns, dry-roasted
1 tablespoon chilli flakes
1 teaspoon salt flakes

1 To make the marinade, whisk barley malt, tamari, vinegar and shaohsing or sherry together in a glass or ceramic bowl large enough to hold the ribs. Using a mortar and pestle, pound garlic, ginger, Sichuan peppercorns, chilli flakes and salt to a paste. Add paste to barley malt mixture and combine well. Add ribs and mix well. Cover and refrigerate for 3 hours or overnight.

2 Preheat oven to 170°C. Place ribs in a roasting tin with marinade and roast for 30 minutes or until ribs are cooked through.

3 Arrange on a serving platter with lime halves. Eat with fingers!

Soy-braised pork belly

For this Chinese favourite, pork belly is slow-braised in dark and light soy sauces, sugar and ginger. The result is shimmering, clean-tasting pork that just melts in the mouth.

750 g pork belly, cut into 1 cm cubes
⅓ cup (80 ml) peanut oil
5 cm piece ginger, finely sliced
½ cup (125 ml) shaohsing wine or dry sherry
¼ cup (60 ml) light soy sauce
2 tablespoons dark soy sauce
1 cup (200 g) brown sugar
1.25 litres water
2 tablespoons brown rice vinegar

1 To remove any impurities from the meat, place pork belly in a large saucepan or stockpot, cover with cold water and bring to the boil. Simmer for 5 minutes, then drain, discarding water. Rinse pork thoroughly under cold running water and drain well.

2 Heat oil in a hot wok until the surface seems to shimmer slightly. Add pork and stir-fry for 3 minutes. Add all other ingredients except vinegar and simmer gently, covered, for 50 minutes or until pork is tender. Stir in vinegar and serve immediately.

Caramelised pork
with ginger and vinegar

When I was cooking in Tibet, I garnished this rich dish with some pickles from the market in Lhasa, but at home you could just use some very finely shredded fresh ginger.

600 g pork belly
2 tablespoons peanut oil
¼ cup (60 ml) shaohsing wine or dry sherry
1 tablespoon brown sugar
3 star anise
1.25 litres water
2 tablespoons Chinese black vinegar
1 tablespoon light soy sauce
1 teaspoon dark soy sauce

MARINADE
1 teaspoon cornflour
1 teaspoon sea salt
¼ cup (60 ml) shaohsing wine or dry sherry
10 cm piece ginger, cut into thin strips

1 To remove any impurities from the meat, place pork belly in a large saucepan or stockpot, cover with cold water and bring to the boil. Simmer for 5 minutes, then drain, discarding water. Rinse pork thoroughly under cold running water and drain well.

2 Cut pork belly into 5 cm × 2.5 cm pieces. Combine marinade ingredients in a large bowl. Add pork and refrigerate for 30 minutes.

3 Heat oil in a hot wok until the surface seems to shimmer slightly. Add pork and stir-fry for 4 minutes.

4 Add remaining ingredients and simmer gently, covered, for 50 minutes or until pork is tender. Serve immediately.

Sung choi bao of pork, ginger and mushrooms

To ensure the success of this dish, fatty pork mince is essential: the higher the fat content of the pork, the more moist and tender the final result will be. And use only iceberg lettuce – its 'meaty' leaves add both texture and structure. This recipe makes more dried Chinese mushrooms than you need here, but they keep for a week in the fridge and are great sliced and added to stir-fries.

4 small perfect leaves iceberg lettuce
2 tablespoons peanut oil
1 tablespoon finely sliced ginger
1 garlic clove, finely diced
⅔ cup fatty pork mince
2 tablespoons roughly chopped salted radish
2 tablespoons roughly chopped pickled
    mustard greens
2 tablespoons finely sliced lup cheong sausage
2 tablespoons shaohsing wine or dry sherry
1 teaspoon white sugar
1 tablespoon light soy sauce
1 tablespoon oyster sauce
¼ teaspoon sesame oil
small handful of carrot, cut into thin strips
handful of bean sprouts
1 tablespoon roughly sliced spring onions
small handful of finely sliced Chinese white cabbage
1 large red chilli, finely sliced on the diagonal
small handful of spring onion cut into fine julienne
    strips, extra
handful of coriander sprigs

BRAISED DRIED CHINESE MUSHROOMS
12 dried Chinese mushrooms
3 cm × 2 cm piece ginger, finely sliced
2 spring onion stems, cut in half lengthways
3 garlic cloves, crushed
2 tablespoons shaohsing wine or dry sherry

1 First make the braised Chinese mushrooms. Soak mushrooms in hot water for 1 hour, ensuring they are fully submerged. When softened, remove stems with scissors and discard.

2 Place mushrooms in medium-sized saucepan, adding enough water to cover. Add ginger, spring onions, garlic and shaohsing or sherry, and bring to the boil. Reduce heat and simmer for 45 minutes or until mushrooms are tender. Allow to cool in the cooking liquid at room temperature. Store in the refrigerator until ready to use.

3 Soak lettuce leaves in cold water for 1 hour, then drain well. Set aside, covered, in the refrigerator.

4 Drain 2 braised dried Chinese mushrooms and slice finely.

5 Heat peanut oil in a hot wok. Add ginger, garlic and pork mince and stir-fry for 1 minute. Add mushrooms, radish, mustard greens and sausage, and continue stir-frying for 5 seconds.

6 Pour in shaohsing or sherry, sugar, soy sauce, oyster sauce and sesame oil, and stir-fry for 2 minutes or until pork is cooked. Toss in carrot, bean sprouts, spring onion and cabbage, and stir to combine, then remove from heat.

7 Serve pork mixture in a bowl set on a large platter, garnished with chilli, spring onion and coriander, and accompanied with the lettuce-leaf cups. To eat, simply spoon pork mixture into lettuce cups, roll up to enclose the pork and eat with your fingers!

Sichuan chicken salad

Sichuan is a province in south-western China that is renowned for its spicy, fiery food. This classic Sichuan-style salad uses Sichuan pepper and salt and dried chilli flakes as the main flavourings; I love how Sichuan pepper and salt makes your tongue go tingly and numb! A very refreshing salad for summer.

1 small cucumber, peeled
100 g White-Cooked Chicken (see page 66),
    breast meat only
3 spring onions, finely chopped
1 stick of celery, finely sliced
small handful of roughly chopped coriander
25 g finely sliced fresh black cloud ear fungus
1 teaspoon light soy sauce
½ teaspoon sesame oil
½ teaspoon dried chilli flakes
¼ teaspoon Sichuan Pepper and
    Salt (see page 138)
1 drop chilli oil

1 Using a vegetable peeler, finely slice cucumber lengthways into ribbons. Cut cucumber into fine strips.

2 Using your fingers, shred chicken meat. Combine chicken and cucumber in a bowl with remaining ingredients and mix thoroughly. Arrange on a platter and sprinkle with a little more Sichuan pepper and salt before serving.

Chicken noodle soup

Chicken noodle soup is one of those comfort dishes that people love – and it is very easy to make if you have some stock in your freezer.

When using vacuum-packed, pre-cooked noodles, I like to rinse them under hot running water before adding them to the soup. This helps to untangle them and also rinses away any excess starch. If you can find fresh Hokkien noodles, I would strongly recommend using them instead. They are made from fresh eggs, so treat them as you would fresh pasta (store in the fridge and use within 3 days), then blanch them in a pot of boiling salted water and drain before adding to your soup.

1 × 450 g packet Hokkien noodles
1.5 litres Rich Chinese Chicken Stock
    (see page 130)
2 tablespoons light soy sauce
1 tablespoon finely sliced ginger
2 teaspoons oyster sauce
1 teaspoon white sugar
½ bunch bok choy
400 g free-range chicken breasts,
    cut widthways into 1 cm slices
1 teaspoon sesame oil
2 spring onions, finely chopped, to garnish
½ cup spring onion, cut into fine julienne strips
2 large red chillies, finely sliced on the diagonal

1 Remove cores from bok choy, cut crossways into 4, then wash thoroughly and drain.

2 Place noodles in a colander and rinse well under hot running water, then drain.

3 Bring stock to the boil in a large heavy-based saucepan. Add soy sauce, ginger, oyster sauce and sugar and stir to combine. Reduce heat, add drained noodles and simmer gently for 30 seconds. Add bok choy and chicken, and simmer for a further 2 minutes or until chicken is just cooked through. Stir in sesame oil, then remove pan from heat.

4 Ladle soup into large bowls and garnish with chopped spring onion. Place spring onion and chilli in a separate bowl and serve alongside soup.

Kylie's white-cooked chicken

My favourite way of cooking chicken Chinese-style is white-cooking, or poaching in a classic Cantonese stock. I have served this simple, nurturing dish in my restaurant for ten years, and I eat it myself at least three times a week. I love it when food makes me feel like this – that is what good food does, it transforms and uplifts your mood.

1 × 1.6 kg free-range chicken
extra virgin olive oil, for drizzling
salt flakes and freshly ground black pepper
1 lemon, cut into wedges
Homemade Chilli Sauce or Ginger, Coriander
 and Spring Onion Dipping Sauce (see page 136),
 to serve

WHITE MASTER STOCK
6 litres cold water
3 cups (750 ml) shaohsing wine or dry sherry
8 spring onions, trimmed and cut in half
 crossways
12 garlic cloves, crushed
2 × 8 cm pieces ginger, finely sliced
½ cup (55 g) salt flakes

1 Place all stock ingredients in a large saucepan or stockpot and bring to the boil. Reduce heat and simmer gently for 40 minutes to allow flavours to infuse.

2 Rinse chicken under cold water. Trim away excess fat from inside and outside cavity, but keep neck, parson's nose and winglets intact. Lower chicken, breast-side down, into simmering stock, ensuring it is fully submerged. Poach chicken gently for exactly 14 minutes. There should be no more than an occasional ripple breaking the surface; adjust the temperature, if necessary, to ensure stock does not reach simmering point again. Immediately remove from heat and allow chicken to steep in stock for 3 hours at room temperature to complete the cooking process. Using tongs, gently remove chicken from stock, being careful not to tear the breast skin. Place chicken on a large plate and allow to cool.

3 Cut chicken into quarters, then drizzle with oil and season with salt and pepper. Garnish with lemon wedges and serve with your choice of sauces.

Kylie's 'radical' roast chicken

Everyone has a favourite roast chicken recipe, and this is mine – a slightly radical version of the classic roast chook, using Chinese double-cooking techniques for a juicy chicken with maximum flavour. The chicken is first 'steamed' in the oven under foil, so it doesn't dry out, then the foil is removed and the heat turned up to give it a lovely crispy skin.

1 × 1.5 kg free-range chicken
½ bunch tarragon, chopped
4 sprigs rosemary, roughly chopped
100 g unsalted butter, sliced
1 head of garlic, cloves separated
10 bay leaves
1 tablespoon sea salt
2 carrots, peeled and cut into wedges
2 small sweet potatoes, peeled and
   cut into wedges
6 kipfler potatoes, peeled and cut into wedges
5 small golden shallots, unpeeled, cut in half
⅓ cup (80 ml) extra virgin olive oil
pinch cracked white pepper
sourdough bread, to serve

1 Preheat oven to 220°C. Rinse chicken under cold water. Trim away excess fat from inside and outside cavity, but keep neck, parson's nose and winglets intact. Tuck wing tips under chicken. Place chicken in a lightly oiled roasting tin, breast-side up.

2 Place tarragon and half the rosemary inside cavity of chicken. Using your hands, carefully separate the skin from the meat over the breast and thighs of the chicken. Place the butter between the skin and the meat, spreading it evenly under the skin.

3 Lightly crush unpeeled garlic cloves and scatter over chicken with bay leaves, salt and remaining rosemary.

4 Place carrots, sweet potatoes, potatoes and shallots around chicken, then drizzle with oil and sprinkle with pepper.

5 Cover roasting tin with foil and roast for 35 minutes. Remove from oven and reduce temperature to 180°C. Remove foil and bake for a further 20 minutes, or until chicken is just cooked through and vegetables are tender. To test chicken, insert a skewer into the thigh and press against the meat – it is cooked when the juices run clear. The skin should be crisp and lightly browned. Remove chicken from oven, cover with foil and leave to rest in a warm place for 10 minutes.

6 Remove chicken from tin and serve with the roast vegetables and some crusty sourdough bread.

Roast cinnamon chicken with lemon and cider vinegar dressing

I love the spicy, tingly flavour of pepperberries. In this dish, it is perfectly offset by the delicious sourness of fresh lemons. Pepperberries are available from selected delicatessens.

1 × 1.5 kg free-range chicken
2 lemons, thickly sliced
8 bay leaves

PEPPERBERRY BUTTER

2 teaspoons dried native Australian
    pepperberries
3 garlic cloves
4 cm piece ginger, finely sliced
1 teaspoon sea salt
½ teaspoon ground cinnamon
1 teaspoon ground cumin
125 g unsalted butter

LEMON AND CIDER VINEGAR DRESSING

1 small lemon
1 garlic clove, finely diced
2 teaspoons sea salt
½ cup (125 ml) extra virgin olive oil
¼ cup (60 ml) lemon juice
1 tablespoon cider vinegar
2 salad onions, finely sliced
2 teaspoons finely grated lemon zest

1 To make the pepperberry butter, pound pepperberries, garlic, ginger, salt and ground spices with a mortar and pestle until well crushed. Mix in the butter until well combined. Set aside.

2 Rinse chicken under cold water. Trim away excess fat from inside and outside cavity, but keep neck, parson's nose and winglets intact. Tuck wing tips under chicken. Place chicken in a lightly oiled roasting tin, breast-side up. Using your hands, ease the breast and thigh skin away from the meat, being careful not to tear the skin. Place half of the reserved butter mixture between the skin and meat of the chicken, spreading it evenly under the skin. Make a couple of cuts in thigh meat to help the heat and flavours penetrate more easily. Rub remaining butter over outside of chicken. Place lemons and bay leaves inside cavity. Cover and refrigerate for 1 hour.

3 Preheat oven to 190°C . Roast chicken, uncovered, for about 1 hour, or until juices run clear and skin is crisp and lightly browned. Remove chicken from oven, cover with foil and leave to rest in a warm place for 10 minutes.

4 Meanwhile, make the dressing. Cut a slice from one end of the lemon and stand the lemon cut-side down on a chopping board. Using a small, sharp knife, cut the skin and pith away, slicing from top to bottom and following the curve of the fruit. Cut the flesh into segments by slicing between the membranes of each section to the centre of the lemon. Pound garlic and salt with a mortar and pestle until you have a rough paste. Mix in the lemon segments and bruise slightly to release juices. Add remaining ingredients, mix well and set aside.

5 Remove chicken from tin, reserving pan juices. Slice chicken and arrange on a platter with lemon slices and bay leaves, drizzling with pan juices. Serve dressing in a bowl on the side.

Braised chicken with vibrant flavours

This can be cooked in advance and then just reheated. The vibrant flavours of this rustic dish come from all over the globe – it's got a little bit of French in it, a little bit of Thai and a little bit of Moroccan. The colours are no less vibrant, with bright red tomatoes and the golden hue of saffron.

Serve with crusty sourdough bread.

small pinch saffron threads
⅓ cup (50 g) plain flour
½ teaspoon sea salt
pinch cracked white pepper
1.5 kg free-range chicken thighs on the bone, skin on
1 cup (250 ml) olive oil
6 cm piece ginger, finely sliced
20 g turmeric, finely diced
10 garlic cloves, crushed
1 tablespoon sea salt, extra
3 small carrots, peeled and cut into chunks
6 small red shallots, peeled
5 small roma (plum) tomatoes
6 bay leaves
100 g palm sugar
¼ cup (60 ml) fish sauce
1 tablespoon finely sliced preserved lemon rind
6 fresh dates, halved and pitted
5 large red chillies, bruised
1 teaspoon ground cumin
1 lime, cut into quarters
½ cup (125 ml) red wine
½ cup (125 ml) sherry vinegar
juice of 1 lime
crusty sourdough bread, to serve

1 Combine saffron with 2 teaspoons of boiling water in a small bowl and set aside.

2 Combine flour with salt and pepper, then toss chicken in seasoned flour to coat thoroughly, shaking away excess. Heat oil in large frying pan and shallow-fry chicken, in batches, until lightly browned on all sides. Remove from pan and drain on kitchen paper. Set aside.

3 Add ginger, turmeric, garlic and extra salt to pan and cook over medium heat, stirring, for about 1 minute, or until fragrant. Add carrots, shallots, tomatoes and bay leaves, stirring well to coat. Add palm sugar and cook, stirring, for a further minute, or until mixture begins to caramelise. Stir in fish sauce and bring to the boil. Add preserved lemon rind, dates, chillies, cumin, lime quarters and reserved saffron water. Stir to combine, then pour in wine and vinegar and simmer over high heat for 2 minutes.

4 Finally, return chicken to the pan and reduce heat. Simmer gently, covered, for about 40 minutes, or until chicken is just cooked through and vegetables are tender. Drizzle chicken with lime juice before serving.

Stir-fried chicken fillets with cashews

This is one of the most frequently ordered dishes in Chinese restaurants. I particularly like the addition of cold, refreshing cucumber right at the last moment.

**800 g free-range chicken thigh fillets,
     cut into 2 cm slices**
1 cucumber
¼ cup (60 ml) vegetable oil
1 cup (150 g) unsalted and roasted cashew nuts
6 garlic cloves, finely diced
2 tablespoons shaohsing wine or dry sherry
2 teaspoons sea salt
4 spring onions, finely chopped

MARINADE
2 tablespoons shaohsing wine or dry sherry
2 tablespoons cornflour
1 tablespoon cold water
1 teaspoon sea salt

1 Combine all marinade ingredients in a bowl, then add chicken and mix well. Cover and refrigerate for 30 minutes.

2 Cut cucumber in half lengthways and scoop out seeds using a spoon. Place cucumber cut-side down on a chopping board, finely slice on the diagonal and set aside.

3 Heat 2 tablespoons of oil in a hot wok until the surface seems to shimmer slightly. Add half the marinated chicken and stir-fry for 1 minute. Remove from wok with a slotted spoon and set aside. Add remaining chicken and stir-fry for 1 minute, then remove from wok and set aside.

4 Add remaining oil to the hot wok, stir in nuts and garlic and stir-fry over medium heat for 30 seconds, stirring constantly to ensure garlic does not burn. Immediately return chicken to the wok and increase heat to high. Pour in shaohsing or sherry and stir-fry for 30 seconds. Add salt and continue to stir-fry for a further 30 seconds or until chicken is lightly browned and just cooked through. Lastly, add reserved cucumber and stir-fry for 10 seconds.

5 Arrange chicken on a platter, garnish with spring onion and serve immediately.

Chilli-salt duck breasts with lemon

This is one of my favourite dishes. It is so simple yet so tasty and impressive – impressive because many people are wary of handling duck. If you feel intimidated about preparing duck (it really is not that difficult), then please try this recipe using duck breasts. You steam the breasts, then roll them in chilli-salt for flavour and deep-fry for texture. Serve with Sichuan pepper and salt and fresh lemon. YUM!

4 × 200 g duck breasts, skin on, trimmed
    of excess fat
2 tablespoons plain flour
3 teaspoons chilli powder
3 teaspoons sea salt
vegetable oil for deep-frying
2 tablespoons Sichuan Pepper and Salt
    (see page 138)
1 large red chilli, finely sliced on the diagonal
¼ cup spring onion cut into fine julienne strips
2 lemons, halved

1 Arrange duck breasts, skin-side up, on a heatproof plate that will fit inside a steamer basket. Place plate inside steamer, position over a deep saucepan or wok of boiling water and steam, covered, for 12 minutes or until duck breasts are half cooked.

2 Meanwhile, in a large bowl, combine flour, chilli powder and salt. Carefully remove plate from steamer basket, transfer duck breasts to a rack and set aside for 25 minutes to cool slightly.

3 Add duck breasts to chilli-salt mixture and toss to coat well, shaking off any excess flour. Heat oil in a large hot wok until the surface seems to shimmer slightly. Add duck breasts and deep-fry for about 2 minutes or until just cooked through and lightly browned, then remove and drain well on kitchen paper.

4 Cut duck on the diagonal into 1 cm slices and arrange on a platter with Sichuan pepper and salt. Garnish with chilli and spring onion and serve immediately with lemon halves.

Crispy-skin duck with blood plum sauce

This is one of the signature dishes at Billy Kwong. I remember a table of four once ordered four ducks because they'd heard so much about it – they wanted a duck each and that was that! If blood plums aren't in season, use blood oranges or regular oranges to add that lovely sourness. Start this the day before.

1 × 1.5 kg fresh duck
2 tablespoons Sichuan Pepper and Salt
   (see page 138)
¼ cup (35 g) plain flour
vegetable oil for deep-frying

BLOOD PLUM SAUCE
1 cup (250 ml) water
1 cup (220 g) white sugar
250 g (about 4) ripe blood plums,
   cut in half
⅔ cup (160 ml) fish sauce
6 star anise
2 cinnamon quills
⅓ cup (80 ml) lime juice

1 Rinse duck under cold water. Trim away excess fat from inside and outside the cavity, but keep neck, parson's nose and winglets intact. Pat dry and rub the skin all over with Sichuan pepper and salt. Cover duck and refrigerate overnight.

2 Transfer duck to a large steamer basket. Place basket over a saucepan of boiling water and steam, covered with a tight-fitting lid, for about 1½ hours, or until duck is cooked through (to test, insert a small knife between leg and breast – the juices should run clear). Using tongs, gently remove duck from steamer and place on a tray, breast-side up, to drain. Allow to cool slightly, then transfer to refrigerator to cool further.

3 Meanwhile, make the blood plum sauce. Combine water and sugar in a small saucepan and bring to the boil. Reduce heat to low and simmer, stirring occasionally, for about 5 minutes, or until slightly reduced. Add plums, fish sauce and spices and simmer for a further minute. Stir through lime juice and remove pan from heat. Keep the sauce warm while you fry the duck.

4 Place cooled duck breast-side up on a chopping board and, using a large knife or cleaver, cut duck in half lengthways through breastbone and backbone. Carefully ease meat away from carcass, leaving thighs, legs and wings intact. Lightly toss duck halves in flour to coat, shaking off any excess. Heat oil in a hot wok until the surface seems to shimmer slightly. Deep-fry duck halves, one at a time, for about 3 minutes, or until well browned and crispy. Using tongs, carefully remove duck from oil and drain well on kitchen paper, then leave to rest in a warm place for 5 minutes.

5 Finally, with a large knife or cleaver, slice the duck, arrange on a platter and spoon over the hot plum sauce.

Roast duck served with fresh figs, shiitake mushrooms and lime

SERVE AS A MAIN MEAL FOR 4

I just can't go past poaching for its gentleness, and the roasting gives the duck a delightful crispiness, in contrast to the sweetness of figs, the velvety texture of fresh shiitake mushrooms and the zing of lime juice.

1 × 1.75 kg fresh duck
2 tablespoons extra virgin olive oil

STOCK
6 litres water
2 cups (500 ml) white wine
3 salad onions, trimmed and sliced
1 small leek, sliced
10 cm piece ginger, finely sliced
12 garlic cloves, crushed
½ bunch flat-leaf parsley, cut in half crossways
¼ cup (55 g) sea salt
1 tablespoon white sugar
1 tablespoon white peppercorns
8 bay leaves

CARAMELISED FIGS AND SHIITAKE MUSHROOMS
4 fresh figs
¼ cup (60 ml) extra virgin olive oil
2 garlic cloves, finely diced
2 teaspoons sea salt
2 tablespoons butter
75 g fresh shiitake mushrooms, stems discarded and caps sliced
3 teaspoons raw sugar
1 tablespoon red wine vinegar
juice of ½ lime
pinch cracked white pepper

1 Place all stock ingredients in a 10-litre stockpot and bring to the boil. Rinse duck under cold water. Trim away excess fat from inside and outside the cavity, but keep neck, parson's nose and winglets intact. Lower duck, breast-side down, into simmering stock, ensuring it is fully submerged. Reduce heat and poach very gently for exactly 25 minutes, skimming stock regularly with a ladle. Remove from heat and allow duck to steep in stock for 2 hours at room temperature to complete the cooking process. Using tongs, gently remove duck from stock and place breast-side up on a tray to drain and cool. Transfer to a chopping board and, with a cleaver or sharp knife, remove winglets and cut duck in half lengthways. Rub skin with a little sea salt and pepper.

2 Preheat oven to 240°C. Heat 1 tablespoon of oil in a heavy-based frying pan and sear duck halves all over until golden brown. Transfer duck to a roasting tin, drizzle the hot oil over its skin and roast for 8 minutes. Remove from oven, cover with foil and leave to rest in a warm place for 10 minutes.

3 Meanwhile, remove stems from figs and cut crossways into 1.5 cm thick slices. Heat oil in a frying pan, add garlic and 1 teaspoon of salt and cook, stirring, for 1 minute. Add butter and mushrooms and fry gently over high heat for about 2 minutes, or until mushrooms begin to soften. Add sugar and cook, stirring, for a further minute, or until sugar is dissolved and begins to caramelise. Add figs, vinegar and remaining teaspoon of salt and gently stir to combine and heat through. Remove from heat, add lime juice and pepper, and set aside.

4 Finally, lay one half of duck on a chopping board. Cut off the wing, then the leg. Remove thigh and breast and cut into slices. Repeat with other half of duck. Arrange duck on a platter and top with the caramelised figs and shiitake mushrooms. Drizzle with remaining oil.

Stir-fried duck breasts with hoisin sauce

Duck and hoisin sauce are a classic match. This dish is perfect served with steamed rice and some freshly cooked Chinese greens.

4 × 200 g duck breasts, skin on,
    trimmed of excess fat
1 teaspoon vegetable oil
¼ cup (60 ml) water
3 spring onions, cut into fine julienne strips

MARINADE
3 garlic cloves, finely diced
¼ cup (60 ml) hoisin sauce
2 tablespoons malt vinegar
2 tablespoons shaohsing wine or dry sherry
1 tablespoon light soy sauce
2 teaspoons white sugar
1 teaspoon five-spice powder
½ teaspoon sesame oil
½ teaspoon sea salt

1 Cut duck breasts on the diagonal into 1 cm slices.

2 Combine all marinade ingredients in a bowl, then add duck breasts and mix well. Cover and refrigerate for 30 minutes.

3 Heat oil in a hot wok, add half the marinated duck and stir-fry for 1 minute. Remove from wok with a slotted spoon and set aside. Add remaining duck with all the marinade juices and stir-fry for 1 minute. Finally, return reserved duck to the wok with water, reduce heat to medium and simmer, uncovered, for 2 minutes or until duck is just tender.

4 Transfer to a serving bowl, garnish with spring onion and serve immediately.

EGGS, VEGETABLES AND TOFU

Soft-boiled eggs with oyster sauce and chilli

Eggs are naturally rich, so they need an intensely flavoured sauce to stand up to them. This dressing is really delicious – the vinegar cuts through the velvety richness of the oyster sauce and the sesame oil adds depth.

6 free-range eggs
1 tablespoon oyster sauce
2 teaspoons malt vinegar
½ teaspoon sesame oil
1 large green chilli, finely sliced on the diagonal
pinch ground white pepper

1 Place eggs in a small saucepan of boiling water and cook for about 4 minutes. Remove eggs from saucepan with a slotted spoon and refresh under cold running water.

2 Meanwhile, combine oyster sauce, vinegar and sesame oil in a small bowl.

3 Carefully peel eggs, cut in half and arrange on a platter. Spoon over oyster sauce mixture, top with chilli and sprinkle with pepper. Serve immediately.

Stir-fried omelette with tomatoes, mushrooms and chilli

A simple dish that's great for an impromptu supper.

6 free-range eggs
2 spring onions, cut into fine julienne strips
1 tablespoon ginger, finely sliced
2 teaspoons light soy sauce
1 teaspoon sea salt
75 g button mushrooms, stems discarded
    and caps sliced
1 small tomato, diced
¼ cup (60 ml) vegetable oil
1 tablespoon oyster sauce
1 large red chilli, finely sliced on the diagonal
2 tablespoons finely chopped spring onion, extra

1 Combine eggs, spring onion, ginger, soy sauce and salt in a bowl and beat lightly with a fork until just combined. Stir in mushrooms and tomato.

2 Heat oil in a hot wok until the surface seems to shimmer slightly. Pour egg mixture into wok and leave to cook on the base of the wok for 30 seconds, without stirring. Using a spatula, fold egg mixture over onto itself and leave to cook for another 30 seconds. Fold over again and leave for 20 seconds or until almost set. Repeat this process once more before lifting omelette from the wok onto a serving platter.

3 Spoon over oyster sauce, sprinkle with chilli and extra spring onion and serve immediately.

Green salad with honey and tamari dressing

I love this simple salad. The luscious golden honey coats the lettuce leaves, and its natural sweetness is balanced out by the salty and sour flavours of the tamari and lemon.

1 head radicchio
1 head baby cos
50 g baby spinach
½ bunch flat-leaf parsley, leaves picked
½ bunch basil, leaves picked
½ bunch dill, leaves picked
½ bunch mint, leaves picked
freshly ground pepper

HONEY AND TAMARI DRESSING
2 tablespoons honey
2 tablespoons tamari
¼ cup (60 ml) extra virgin olive oil
juice of 1 lemon

1 Trim lettuce. Soak in cold water with spinach and herbs, then spin dry.

2 Place all dressing ingredients in a bowl and whisk well. Combine with lettuce and herbs and toss. Season with pepper and serve.

Chinese-style lettuce salad

I created this simple salad in celebration of iceberg lettuce – it's so meaty, with so much texture and structure. The dressing is a balance of salty, sweet and sour.

½ iceberg lettuce
100 g baby spinach leaves
large handful of mint leaves
3 spring onions, cut into fine julienne strips
pinch Sichuan Pepper and Salt (see page 138)

DRESSING
100 ml extra virgin olive oil
¼ cup (60 ml) malt vinegar
2 tablespoons light soy sauce
1 garlic clove, finely diced
1 teaspoon white sugar

1 Remove leaves from lettuce and wash well. Roughly tear leaves into large pieces, then place in a large bowl with spinach, mint and spring onion and refrigerate, covered, for 1 hour.

2 Meanwhile, to make the dressing, place all ingredients in a small bowl and stir to combine.

3 Pour dressing over chilled salad leaves and toss well. Arrange on a platter, sprinkle with Sichuan pepper and salt and serve immediately.

Chickpea and tomato salad with Asian dressing

Chickpeas are high in protein and quite filling, so I always try to match them with a piquant dressing. This Asian-flavoured mayonnaise-like dressing coats every chickpea, and the fresh herbs bring the salad alive.

1 cup (200 g) dried chickpeas, soaked overnight
    in plenty of cold water
1 small red onion, finely sliced
1 teaspoon salt flakes
1 teaspoon brown sugar
1 tablespoon brown rice vinegar
2 small tomatoes, roughly diced
1 small carrot, peeled and cut into ribbons
    using a vegetable peeler
handful of flat-leaf parsley leaves
handful of basil leaves
juice of 1 lemon

DRESSING
1 free-range egg yolk
1 teaspoon brown sugar
1 tablespoon tamari
1 tablespoon brown rice vinegar
½ cup (125 ml) extra virgin olive oil

1 Drain chickpeas and place in a saucepan covered with cold water. Bring to the boil, then simmer over a low–medium heat for approximately 45 minutes or until tender. Allow the chickpeas to cool in their cooking water, then drain. Set aside.

2 Place onion in a bowl with salt and sugar, mix thoroughly and set aside for 30 minutes. Add vinegar and mix well. Set aside.

3 To make the dressing, whisk egg yolk and sugar together in a bowl until smooth and fluffy. Add tamari and vinegar, whisking to combine. Slowly whisk in oil until the dressing is smooth and emulsified.

4 To serve, place onion and all remaining ingredients in a bowl, pour over the dressing and mix well.

Stir-fried snow peas with garlic

These crunchy snow peas are simply and quickly cooked to retain all their natural vitality.

2 tablespoons vegetable oil
½ teaspoon sea salt
250 g snow peas, trimmed
2 garlic cloves, lightly crushed
1 garlic clove, extra, finely diced
¼ teaspoon white sugar
**½ cup (125 ml) Rich Chinese Chicken
   Stock (see page 130)**
¼ teaspoon sesame oil

1 Heat vegetable oil in a hot wok until the surface seems to shimmer slightly. Add salt and snow peas and stir-fry for 2 minutes. Immediately add crushed and diced garlic and stir-fry for 1 minute, stirring constantly to ensure garlic does not burn.

2 Add sugar to wok and stir-fry for 10 seconds. Pour in stock and simmer for 2 minutes or until snow peas are tender. Lastly, add sesame oil and serve immediately.

Stir-fried eggplant with Linda's homemade chilli sauce

You only need a couple of tablespoons of Linda's homemade chilli sauce in this recipe, but the rest will keep for at least a week in the refrigerator, and is great for adding a kick to stir-fries.

6 Japanese eggplants (aubergines)
1 teaspoon sea salt
2 tablespoons peanut oil
½ teaspoon Sichuan Pepper and Salt
  (see page 138)

LINDA'S CHILLI SAUCE
½ cup (125 ml) peanut oil
6 large red chillies, roughly chopped
10 garlic cloves, roughly chopped
7 cm piece ginger, roughly chopped
1 tablespoon light soy sauce
1 tablespoon chopped coriander leaves
  and stems

1 To make the chilli sauce, heat oil in a wok until the surface seems to shimmer slightly. Add chilli, garlic and ginger and stir constantly over medium heat for 5 minutes. Reduce heat to low and cook, still stirring, for a further 5 minutes. Stir through soy sauce and coriander. The chilli sauce can be used straight away, or allowed to cool and then stored in an airtight container in the refrigerator for up to 1 week.

2 Cut eggplant into 2.5 cm slices on the diagonal, then sprinkle both sides with salt and spread on a tray in one layer. Set aside for 1 hour.

3 Rinse eggplant in a colander under cold running water. Drain and pat dry with kitchen paper.

4 Heat oil in a wok until the surface seems to shimmer slightly. Add eggplant and stir-fry over high heat for 3 minutes. Reduce heat to low and stir-fry for a further 3 minutes.

5 Add 2 tablespoons chilli sauce and stir-fry for 1 minute. Serve immediately, sprinkled with Sichuan pepper and salt.

Spicy dry-fried green beans with hoisin sauce and garlic

A Billy Kwong staple, this dish was created by Chris, who used to work at the restaurant – he cooked it for staff dinner one evening and it has never been off the menu since! The wilted beans soak up the flavours of the hoisin sauce and the nutty, caramelised garlic, while the salt perfectly balances the richness.

vegetable oil for deep-frying
150 g green beans
1½ tablespoons hoisin sauce
½ teaspoon finely diced garlic
¼ teaspoon sea salt
¼ teaspoon vegetable oil, extra
2 large red chillies, cut in half lengthways
    and seeds scraped

1 Heat oil in a hot wok until the surface seems to shimmer slightly. Deep-fry beans for 1–2 minutes or until just tender and slightly wilted. Using a slotted spoon, remove from oil, drain on kitchen paper and set aside.

2 Carefully drain hot oil from wok and wipe clean with kitchen paper.

3 In the clean wok, combine hoisin sauce, garlic, salt, extra oil and chilli. Toss in reserved beans and turn up heat to high. Stir-fry beans for 2–3 minutes, coating them in the sauce. Serve immediately, with a little extra salt, if desired.

Chinese broccoli with oyster sauce

Otherwise known as 'gai lan', these are the Chinese greens you'll know from yum cha, where they're wheeled around on big steel trolleys, ready to be plunged into boiling water and drizzled with oyster sauce. This recipe is incredibly easy but the secret, as with most Chinese vegetable dishes, is to cook it at the last minute.

1 bunch Chinese broccoli (gai lan)
1 tablespoon vegetable oil
2 tablespoons oyster sauce
dash of sesame oil
1 tablespoon peanut oil

1 Trim 5 cm from ends of broccoli, cut bunch crossways into 3 lengths and wash thoroughly.

2 Fill a large saucepan with water and bring to the boil. Stir in vegetable oil, then add broccoli and simmer until bright green and tender – this should take about 1 minute. Using tongs, immediately remove broccoli from water and place on a platter. Drizzle with oyster sauce and sesame oil.

3 Heat peanut oil in a small frying pan until moderately hot and carefully pour over broccoli. Serve immediately.

Stir-fried carrots, zucchini and celery

Three humble ingredients lightly cooked – healthy, tasty and balanced.

2 carrots, peeled
2 zucchini (courgettes)
2 tablespoons peanut oil
2 sticks of celery, finely sliced on the diagonal
1 red onion, roughly sliced
6 ginger slices
3 garlic cloves, crushed
¼ cup (60 ml) shaohsing wine or dry sherry
2 tablespoons light soy sauce
1 tablespoon malt vinegar
2 teaspoons white sugar
½ teaspoon sesame oil

1 Cut carrots and zucchini in half lengthways and then into 5 mm slices on the diagonal.

2 Heat peanut oil in a hot wok until the surface seems to shimmer slightly. Add carrot, zucchini, celery, onion, ginger and garlic and stir-fry for 2 minutes. Add shaohsing or sherry and stir-fry for 10 seconds. Lastly, add soy sauce, vinegar, sugar and sesame oil and stir-fry for a further 2 minutes or until vegetables are just tender. Serve immediately.

Deep-fried silken tofu with Sichuan pepper and salt

When cooked properly, the tofu should boast a crunchy, golden outside and a silky, piping-hot inside. The salty, aromatic flavour of Sichuan pepper and salt brings the tofu to life, as does the refreshing contrast of the sour lemon.

Eat the fried tofu immediately after cooking, as it becomes moist and loses its crunch when it cools.

1 × 300 g packet silken tofu
vegetable oil for deep-frying
⅓ cup (50 g) cornflour
1 teaspoon Sichuan Pepper and Salt (see page 138)
1 lemon, cut into pieces

1 Gently remove tofu from packet and invert on a plate. Carefully slice into 6 cubes, draining off any excess liquid.

2 Heat oil in a hot wok until the surface seems to shimmer slightly. Lightly coat tofu pieces in cornflour and, using a fish slice, carefully lower into the hot oil. (It is important not to coat the tofu before heating the oil, or it will become very moist and sticky.) Deep-fry tofu until golden brown, remove with a slotted spoon and drain well on kitchen paper.

3 Arrange tofu on a platter and serve immediately, sprinkled with Sichuan pepper and salt and accompanied by lemon pieces.

Stir-fried tofu with vegetables

I must stress the importance of slicing ingredients finely when stir-frying: not only do they cook correctly, but the overall look is wild – so much movement and colour!

1 small carrot, peeled
1 zucchini (courgette)
½ red capsicum (pepper)
2 tablespoons peanut oil
1 × 200 g packet five-spice pressed tofu,
    finely sliced
1 red onion, finely sliced
1 tablespoon finely sliced ginger
¼ cup (60 ml) shaohsing wine or dry sherry
2 teaspoons white sugar
2 teaspoons light soy sauce
2 teaspoons malt vinegar
1 teaspoon oyster sauce
½ teaspoon sesame oil
9 spring onions, cut into fine julienne strips

1 Cut carrot and zucchini in half lengthways, then finely slice on the diagonal. Remove seeds and membranes from pepper and cut into fine slices.

2 Heat oil in a hot wok until the surface seems to shimmer slightly. Add carrot, tofu, onion and ginger and stir-fry for 1 minute. Add shaohsing or sherry, zucchini, capsicum and sugar and stir-fry for 1 minute. Pour in soy sauce, vinegar, oyster sauce and sesame oil and stir-fry for a further minute or until vegetables are just tender. Toss in spring onion, stir-fry for 10 seconds, then remove from heat.

3 Transfer to a shallow bowl and serve immediately.

Deep-fried tofu with
black bean and chilli sauce

The substantial, robust flavours of black bean and chilli sauce work miracles with tofu simply coated in flour and then deep-fried.

1 × 300 g packet silken tofu
vegetable oil for deep-frying
⅓ cup (50 g) plain flour
pinch Sichuan Pepper and Salt (see page 138)

BLACK BEAN AND CHILLI SAUCE
1 tablespoon vegetable oil
½ small red onion, finely sliced
1 tablespoon finely sliced ginger
2 small garlic cloves, roughly chopped
2 teaspoons salted black beans
1 tablespoon shaohsing wine or dry sherry
2 teaspoons light soy sauce
2 teaspoons oyster sauce
2 teaspoons white sugar
2 teaspoons malt vinegar
¼ teaspoon sesame oil
1 large red chilli, finely sliced on the diagonal
¼ red capsicum (pepper), seeds and membranes
    removed, cut into fine slices
⅓ cup (80 ml) water

1 To make the black bean and chilli sauce, add oil to a hot wok, add onion, ginger, garlic and black beans and stir-fry over high heat for 1 minute, stirring constantly to ensure black beans do not burn. Add shaohsing or sherry and stir-fry for 20 seconds, then add soy sauce, oyster sauce, sugar, vinegar and sesame oil and stir-fry for 30 seconds. Toss in chilli and capsicum and stir-fry for 30 seconds. Lastly pour in water and simmer for a further 30 seconds.

2 Gently remove tofu from packet and invert onto a plate. Carefully slice into 6 cubes, draining off any excess liquid.

3 Heat oil in a hot wok until the surface seems to shimmer slightly. Lightly coat tofu pieces in flour, and, using a spatula, carefully lower into the hot oil. (It is important not to coat the tofu before heating the oil, or it will become very moist and sticky.) Deep-fry tofu for about 4 minutes or until lightly browned and crisp. Remove with a slotted spoon and drain well on kitchen paper.

4 Arrange tofu in a shallow bowl and spoon sauce over the top. Sprinkle with Sichuan pepper and salt and serve immediately.

Steamed silken tofu with stir-fried spinach

There is nothing more delicious than stir-fried tender spinach with garlic! This dish could not be easier, yet it is so cleansing and pure. By steaming blocks of silken tofu in this way, you'll experience the true delight of its creamy, custard-like texture.

1 × 300 g packet silken tofu
2 tablespoons vegetable oil
½ teaspoon sea salt
1 bunch spinach, trimmed and cut
    crossways into 5 pieces
2 garlic cloves, finely chopped
¼ cup (60 ml) water
2 teaspoons light soy sauce
1 teaspoon white sugar
¼ teaspoon sesame oil
pinch ground white pepper

1 Gently remove tofu from packet and invert into a shallow heatproof bowl that will fit inside a steamer basket. Carefully cut tofu crossways into 8 equal slices. Place bowl inside steamer, position over a deep saucepan or wok of boiling water and steam, covered, for about 6 minutes or until heated through. Carefully remove bowl from steamer and drain away excess liquid. Using a spatula, transfer tofu to a shallow serving bowl.

2 Meanwhile, heat vegetable oil in a hot wok until the surface seems to shimmer slightly. Add salt and stir-fry for 10 seconds. Toss in spinach and garlic and stir-fry for 1 minute. Add water, soy sauce and sugar and stir-fry for a further minute or until leaves are wilted and stalks are just tender. Lastly, stir through sesame oil and remove from heat.

3 Arrange spinach over hot tofu and drizzle with wok juices. Sprinkle with pepper and serve immediately.

RICE, DUMPLINGS AND NOODLES

Steamed rice

I find that this absorption method always, always works – and the result is beautiful, fluffy white rice!

1⅓ cups (265 g) jasmine rice
2⅔ cups (660 ml) water

1 Place rice in a sieve and rinse under running water until water runs clear. Combine water and rice in a medium-sized heavy-based saucepan. Bring to the boil, then immediately cover with a tight-fitting lid and reduce heat to as low as possible. Cook, covered, for 10 minutes. Do not remove lid during cooking.

2 Remove saucepan from the heat and stand, covered, for 10 minutes. Fluff rice with a fork before serving.

Delicious fried rice

Fried rice is one of those lovely comforting foods that everyone in the world seems to like. Somehow all these rogue ingredients have crept into restaurant versions over the years, such as corn, peas, ham and the like. I find the trick with fried rice is to keep it really simple and traditional – just some really fresh and fluffy eggs, onion, bacon or Chinese sausage, ginger and some spring onions. All rice dishes can be served with a side bowl of light soy sauce and finely sliced chillies.

One hint – yesterday's rice always makes the best fried rice.

⅓ cup (80 ml) peanut oil
4 free-range eggs, beaten
1 tablespoon peanut oil, extra
1½ tablespoons finely chopped ginger
4 garlic cloves, diced
1 brown onion, finely diced
2 rindless bacon rashers or 1 Chinese sausage,
  roughly chopped
1 teaspoon white sugar
2 tablespoons shaohsing wine or dry sherry
5 cups (550 g) cooked medium-grain white rice
1 tablespoon oyster sauce
9 spring onions, cut into fine julienne strips
3 teaspoons Maggi seasoning
¼ teaspoon sesame oil
2 spring onions, extra, finely sliced on the diagonal
¼ cup (60 ml) light soy sauce
½ large red chilli, finely sliced on the diagonal

1 Heat oil in a hot wok until the surface seems to shimmer slightly. Pour beaten eggs into wok and cook for about 1 minute, lightly scrambling them and rotating the wok to ensure even cooking. When almost cooked through, carefully remove omelette from wok with a fish slice and drain on kitchen paper. Set aside.

2 Wipe out wok with kitchen paper, add extra oil and stir-fry ginger and garlic for 1 minute, or until very aromatic. Add onion and stir-fry for 2 minutes, or until lightly browned and tender. Add bacon or sausage and stir-fry for a further minute, or until lightly browned. Stir in sugar and shaohsing or sherry, then stir-fry for 30 seconds. Finally, add rice, reserved omelette, oyster sauce, spring onion, Maggi seasoning and sesame oil. Stir-fry for 3 minutes, or until rice is heated through. Roughly chop omelette into smaller pieces as you stir.

3 Divide rice between individual bowls and garnish with extra spring onion. Combine soy sauce and chilli in a small bowl and serve on the side.

Prawn wontons with spring onion, ginger and vinegar dressing

If you boil rather than deep-fry wontons, you'll end up with little soft pillows. The dressing is inspired by sauces made in the Sichuan province of China and the coriander, spring onion and ginger fill it with lots of chewy, yummy bits!

2½ tablespoons light soy sauce
2 tablespoons finely sliced coriander roots
    and stems
2 tablespoons finely diced ginger
2 tablespoons finely sliced spring onion
2 tablespoons kecap manis
2 tablespoons malt vinegar
¼ teaspoon chilli oil
dash of sesame oil

WONTONS
9 uncooked prawns
1 tablespoon roughly chopped coriander leaves
1 tablespoon finely chopped spring onion
1½ teaspoons finely diced ginger
1 teaspoon shaohsing wine or dry sherry
1 teaspoon light soy sauce
1 teaspoon oyster sauce
¼ teaspoon white sugar
¼ teaspoon sesame oil
16 fresh wonton wrappers, about 7 cm square

1 Combine soy sauce, coriander, ginger, spring onion, kecap manis, vinegar and both oils in a bowl and set aside.

2 For the wontons, peel and devein the prawns, then dice the meat – you should have about 150 g diced prawn meat. Combine prawn meat with remaining ingredients except wonton wrappers in a bowl. Cover and refrigerate for 30 minutes.

3 Next, fill and shape the wontons. Place a rounded teaspoon of the filling in the centre of a wonton wrapper, then dip your finger in water and moisten the bottom edge of the wrapper. Fold the wrapper in half towards you to enclose the filling and press lightly to seal. Hold the wonton lengthways between your hands with the folded edge facing down. Fold the sealed edge of the wonton back on itself, then lightly moisten one corner of the folded edge with water. Finally, taking the two ends in your fingers, bring them together with a twisting action, and press lightly to join. Repeat with remaining filling and wrappers

4 Bring a large saucepan of water to the boil. Drop wontons, in batches, into the water and cook for 2 minutes or until they are just cooked. (To test, remove one using a slotted spoon and cut into it with a sharp knife to see if the prawns are cooked through.) Remove wontons with a slotted spoon and drain. Repeat process with remaining wontons.

5 Arrange wontons on a platter and serve immediately, drizzled with dressing.

Stir-fried Hokkien noodles with chicken and oyster mushrooms

My mother insists that chicken thigh fillets are better for stir-frying than chicken breast fillets as they remain more moist and tender – and she is right! I like to lightly marinate the chicken before cooking, to give the dish an overall depth of flavour and help create a lovely, rich sauce.

400 g free-range chicken thigh fillets,
    cut into 2 cm slices
¼ cup (60 ml) vegetable oil
150 g oyster mushrooms, stems discarded
1 small red onion, cut in half and then into
    thick wedges
4 spring onions, trimmed and cut into
    10 cm lengths
12 slices ginger
1 × 450 g packet fresh Hokkien noodles
2 tablespoons light soy sauce
2 tablespoons shaohsing wine or dry sherry
1 tablespoon white sugar
1 tablespoon malt vinegar
½ teaspoon sesame oil
small handful of coriander sprigs
2 large red chillies, finely sliced on the diagonal
2 tablespoons light soy sauce, extra

MARINADE
1 tablespoon white sugar
1 tablespoon light soy sauce
1 tablespoon shaohsing wine or dry sherry
½ teaspoon sesame oil

1 Combine all marinade ingredients in a bowl, then add chicken and mix well. Cover and refrigerate for 30 minutes.

2 Heat 2 tablespoons of the oil in a hot wok until the surface seems to shimmer slightly. Add chicken and stir-fry for 1 minute. Remove from wok and set aside.

3 Add remaining oil to hot wok with mushrooms, onion, spring onion and ginger and stir-fry for 1 minute or until onion is lightly browned. Toss in noodles, reserved chicken, soy sauce, shaohsing or sherry, sugar, vinegar and sesame oil and stir-fry for a further 2 minutes or until chicken is just cooked through and noodles are hot.

4 Arrange the noodles in bowls and top with coriander sprigs. Serve immediately with a small bowl of sliced chilli mixed with the extra soy sauce.

Kylie's Hokkien noodles

My Hokkien noodles are, I guess, like me – they're a bit radical! They've got all my favourite ingredients in them: Chinese black vinegar, luscious kecap manis, sesame oil, shaohsing wine and a little bit of sugar, as well as pickles and mint. And I just love eating them with chillies. Again, you can see the recurring theme in Asian cooking of each dish being a balance of sweet, sour, salty and hot flavours. I like to leave the skin on, to keep the chicken moist. You can store any leftover pickles in an airtight container in the refrigerator.

5 tablespoons roughly chopped ginger
4 garlic cloves, crushed
⅓ cup (80 ml) kecap manis
2 tablespoons Chinese black vinegar
2 tablespoons Maggi seasoning
⅔ cup (160 ml) shaohsing wine or dry sherry
2 free-range chicken breast fillets, thickly sliced
    on the diagonal
600 g fresh Hokkien noodles
2 tablespoons peanut oil
1 small cucumber, peeled and finely sliced
    on the diagonal
¾ cup (100 g) carrot and onion
    pickles (see below)
2 tablespoons oyster sauce
⅔ cup (75 g) fresh black cloud ear fungus
small handful of mint leaves
pinch Sichuan Pepper and Salt (see page 138)

CARROT AND ONION PICKLES
2 small carrots
1 small white onion
1 tablespoon white sugar
2 teaspoons sea salt
½ cup (125 ml) rice wine vinegar
2 teaspoons fish sauce

1 To make the carrot and onion pickles, use a mandoline or a very sharp knife to finely slice carrots lengthways into ribbons. Cut onion in half lengthways and finely slice in the same way. Place carrot and onion in a bowl, sprinkle with sugar and salt, and mix well. Cover with plastic wrap and leave to stand for 15 minutes. Add vinegar and fish sauce and stand for a further 15 minutes, or until the vegetables are slightly softened and pickled.

2 Pound ginger and garlic with a mortar and pestle until you have a coarse paste. Combine half the paste in a bowl with kecap manis, vinegar, Maggi seasoning and half the shaohsing. Add chicken and, using your hands, mix thoroughly. Cover and refrigerate for 1 hour.

3 Meanwhile, blanch noodles in boiling salted water until al dente – about 4 minutes. Drain, refresh in cold water, then thoroughly drain again and set aside.

4 Heat oil in a hot wok until the surface seems to shimmer slightly. Stir-fry chicken for about 2 minutes, or until almost cooked. Remove from wok and set aside. Add remaining ginger and garlic paste, cucumber and noodles and stir-fry for 1 minute. Add remaining shaohsing, pickled vegetables, oyster sauce and mushrooms and stir-fry for a further minute. Return chicken to wok and stir-fry until chicken is just cooked through and noodles are hot.

5 Stir mint leaves through noodles. Arrange in bowls, sprinkle with Sichuan pepper and salt, and serve immediately.

Stir-fried rice noodles with black beans, chillies and coriander

The silky texture of rice noodles and the robust flavours of black beans, chilli and coriander make for a simple yet very more-ish dish.

500 g fresh rice noodle sheets
¼ cup (60 ml) peanut oil
2 tablespoons salted black beans
small handful of finely chopped coriander
    roots and stems
2 large red chillies, finely chopped
2 tablespoons light soy sauce
1 tablespoon dark soy sauce
1 teaspoon sesame oil

1 Cut noodle sheets into 1 cm strips and carefully separate them.

2 Heat peanut oil in a hot wok until the surface seems to shimmer slightly. Add black beans, coriander and chilli and stir-fry for 1½ minutes, stirring constantly to ensure the black beans do not burn. Toss in rice noodles and stir-fry for 1 minute.

3 Add remaining ingredients and stir-fry for a further 3 minutes or until noodles are heated through. Serve immediately.

STOCKS, SAUCES AND SALTS

Rich Chinese chicken stock

By using a whole chicken you can create a deep, richly flavoured and textured stock that is perfect for a hearty winter's soup. I always remind my staff that the key to good stock-making is having the best-quality ingredients. Stocks influence so many dishes; it is as if a little of their 'spirit' is being released into each dish they touch, whether it be a soup or a stir-fry. Quality is of the utmost importance.

1 × 1.8 kg free-range chicken
4 litres cold water
10 spring onions, trimmed and cut in
half crossways
1 large red onion, roughly chopped
7 cm piece ginger, sliced
10 garlic cloves, crushed

1 Rinse chicken and trim away excess fat from inside and outside cavity. Cut chicken into about 10 pieces and place in a large stockpot, along with all the remaining ingredients. Bring to the boil, then reduce heat to a gentle simmer, skimming the surface with a ladle to remove any impurities.

2 Turn down heat until surface of the stock is barely moving and cook for 2 hours, skimming as required.

3 Remove stock from heat and discard chicken pieces. Strain stock through muslin (or a clean Chux) and store, covered, in the refrigerator for up to 3 days or in the freezer for 2–3 months.

Chinese fish stock

This stock is beautiful, delicate and refined. I prefer to use sweet-flavoured, white-fleshed, delicate fish such as snapper, bream, flathead, perch, sea bass, halibut and cod. I find that oily fish like mackerel, herring and sardine can be far too overpowering for stock. Ask your fishmonger for some fresh fish carcasses to make this.

600 g fresh fish carcasses, heads and tails
3 litres cold water
6 spring onions, trimmed and cut into 5 cm lengths
1 small white onion, finely diced
handful of finely sliced coriander roots and stems
7 cm piece ginger, sliced
5 garlic cloves, crushed

1 Wash fish carcasses, heads and tails well under cold running water. Place all ingredients in a large stockpot and bring to the boil. Reduce heat to a gentle simmer, skimming the surface with a ladle to remove any impurities.

2 Turn down heat until surface of the stock is barely moving and cook for 30 minutes, skimming as required.

3 Remove stock from stove and discard fish carcasses, heads and tails. Strain stock through muslin (or a clean Chux) and store, covered, in the refrigerator for up to 2 days or in the freezer for 1 month.

Chinese vegetable stock

Gently frying the vegetables with sea salt helps to bring out their natural flavours and colours. By using the freshest vegetables, you can create a stock that is full of vibrancy and life. This is great to have in the freezer: it is excellent as a soup base and adds depth of flavour to stir-fries.

1 tablespoon vegetable oil
2 red onions, finely diced
7 cm piece ginger, sliced
10 garlic cloves, crushed
1 tablespoon sea salt
3 carrots, peeled and sliced
6 sticks celery, sliced
10 spring onions, trimmed and cut into
    5 cm lengths
large handful of finely sliced coriander
    roots and stems
6 litres cold water

1 Heat oil in a large stockpot, add onions, ginger, garlic and salt, and fry over high heat for 1 minute. Add carrots, celery, spring onions and coriander, reduce heat and fry gently, stirring often, for a further 3 minutes or until vegetables are very lightly browned.

2 Add water to the pot and bring to the boil. Reduce heat to a gentle simmer, skimming the surface with a ladle to remove any impurities.

3 Turn down heat until surface of the stock is barely moving and cook for 1 hour, skimming as required.

4 Remove stock from stove, strain through muslin (or a clean Chux) and store, covered, in the refrigerator for up to 3 days or in the freezer for 2–3 months.

Homemade chilli sauce (right)

Both of these sauces taste great with my White-Cooked Chicken (see page 66).

4 long red chillies, roughly chopped
3 garlic cloves, roughly chopped
7 cm piece ginger, roughly chopped
¼ cup (60 ml) peanut oil
1 teaspoon brown sugar
1 tablespoon tamari

1 Pound chilli, garlic and ginger to a paste using a mortar and pestle.

2 Heat oil in a wok until moderately hot. Add paste and cook, stirring constantly, for about 3 minutes. Add sugar and stir for 1 minute or until sugar caramelises, then stir through tamari. Reduce heat to low and cook, still stirring, for a further 5 minutes. The chilli sauce can be used straight away, or allowed to cool and then stored in an airtight container in the fridge for up to a week.

Ginger, coriander and spring onion dipping sauce (left)

2 × 8 cm pieces ginger, roughly chopped
1 bunch spring onions, mostly dark green
    ends, finely sliced
1 bunch coriander, stems and roots only,
    finely sliced
¾ teaspoon salt flakes
pinch of white pepper
¾ cup (180 ml) peanut oil

1 Pound ginger, spring onion, coriander and salt to a paste using a mortar and pestle. Transfer to a heatproof bowl, add pepper and mix well.

2 Heat oil in a small frying pan until moderately hot. Carefully pour over the paste, scalding the ingredients to release their fragrance and aroma. Mix well.

Sichuan pepper and salt

I love using this to pep up stir-fries, salads and braises – it adds just the right amount of warmth and saltiness with a light citrus note.

1 tablespoon Sichuan peppercorns
3 tablespoons salt flakes

1 Dry-roast the Sichuan peppercorns and salt flakes in a heavy-based saucepan or wok. When the peppercorns begin to 'pop' and become aromatic, immediately remove them from the heat.

2 Allow to cool, then grind to a powder in a mortar and pestle or spice grinder. Store in an airtight container.

Chilli salt

I like to place a small bowl of this on the table, so people can add as much or as little as they like – it's especially good with grilled meats.

2 tablespoons salt flakes
1 tablespoon dried chilli flakes

1 Dry-roast salt flakes and chilli flakes in a heavy-based saucepan or wok until fragrant, stirring or tossing to combine.

2 Allow to cool, then store in an airtight container.

Index

LANTERN

Published by the Penguin Group
Penguin Group (Australia)
707 Collins Street, Melbourne, Victoria 3008, Australia
(a division of Pearson Australia Group Pty Ltd)
Penguin Group (USA) Inc.
375 Hudson Street, New York, New York 10014, USA
Penguin Group (Canada)
90 Eglinton Avenue East, Suite 700, Toronto,
Canada ON M4P 2Y3
(a division of Pearson Penguin Canada Inc.)
Penguin Books Ltd
80 Strand, London WC2R 0RL, England
Penguin Ireland
25 St Stephen's Green, Dublin 2, Ireland
(a division of Penguin Books Ltd)
Penguin Books India Pvt Ltd
11 Community Centre, Panchsheel Park, New Delhi –
110 017, India
Penguin Group (NZ)
67 Apollo Drive, Rosedale, Auckland 0632,
New Zealand
(a division of Pearson New Zealand Ltd)
Penguin Books (South Africa) (Pty) Ltd
Rosebank Office Park, Block D, 181 Jan Smuts Avenue,
Parktown North, Johannesburg 2196,
South Africa

Penguin Books Ltd, Registered Offices: 80 Strand,
London, WC2R 0RL, England

First published by Penguin Group (Australia), 2012

10 9 8 7 6 5 4 3

Text copyright © Kylie Kwong 2012

Photographs copyright © Earl Carter 2012
(pages 14, 25, 26, 31, 33, 45, 49, 52, 63, 64, 74, 77, 82, 86,
89, 93, 101, 103, 104, 109, 111, 112, 117, 121, 122, 131, 133, 134)

Photographs copyright © Simon Griffiths 2012
(pages 2, 6, 7, 17, 19, 35, 37, 38, 39, 46, 55, 57, 59, 67, 91,
95, 98, 127, 137, 139, 140)

Photographs copyright © David Matheson 2012
(pages 11, 21, 29, 61, 97, 107)

Photographs copyright © Ian Wallace 2012
(pages 12, 23, 43, 50, 69, 71, 73, 79, 81, 119, 125)

Design by Lantern Studio © Penguin Group (Australia)
Typeset in Alright Sans and Adobe Caslon
by Post Pre-press Group, Brisbane, Queensland
Colour reproduction by Splitting Image, Clayton, Victoria
Printed in China by Everbest Printing Co Ltd

National Library of Australia
Cataloguing-in-Publication data:

Kwong, Kylie.
Lantern cookery classics : Kylie Kwong / Kylie Kwong

9781921383182 (pbk.)
Includes index.

Cooking.

641.5

penguin.com.au/lantern